CLIMATE CHANGE:
OUR IMPACT ON EARTH

RENEWABLE ENERGY

by

Harriet Brundle

KidHaven
PUBLISHING

Published in 2018 by
KidHaven Publishing, an Imprint of Greenhaven Publishing, LLC
353 3rd Avenue
Suite 255
New York, NY 10010

Designer: Drue Rintoul
Editor: Charlie Ogden

Photo Credits
Abbreviations: l-left, r-right, b-bottom, t-top, c-center, m-middle.

Front Cover: bl – andrea crisante. tr – yanugkelid. t – photo5963_shutter. tl – Kucher Serhii. b – Krasowit.
br – Dusit. 4b – Matt Berger. 4br – spaxiax. 4l – Iakov Kalinin. 5br – Elnur. 6t – huyangshu. 6b –
project1photography. 7t – Durk Talsma. 7b – Balu. 8b – Andrey tiyk. 8–9c – pryzmat. 9t – Jesus Keller.
10b – majeczka. 11t – Rudmer Zwerver. 12b – Diyana Dimitrova. 13m – RoschetzkyProductions. 14t –
irisphoto1. 14–15bc – Sky Light Pictures. 15tl – Alex Mit. 16bl – Scanrail1. 16r – ANCH. 17t – Mut Hardman.
17m – Mut Hardman. 17b – Ansebach. 18bl – iamnong. 18r – Leona Kali. 19tr – Burben. 19b – By Gringer
(talk) 23:52, 10 February 2009 (UTC) (vector data from [1]) [Public domain], via Wikimedia Commons. 20b
– Carlos Caetano. 20tr – weedezign. 21tl – Amy Johansson. 21br – nikkytok. 22b – Galyna Andrushko.
23t – v.schlichting. 23m – Matej Kastelic. 24b – jiawangkun. 25t – humphery. 25m – stephen rudolph.
25b – Zoran Karapancev. 26r – Chris Haye. 26b – Ozgur Coskun. 27tl – Daisy Daisy. 27b – mRGB.
28t – antoniodiaz. 28m – Diego Cervo. 28b – wk1003mike. 29t – bikeriderlondon. 29m – Still AB. 29b –
Poznyakov. Images are courtesy of Shutterstock.com, with thanks to Getty Images, Thinkstock Photo, and
iStockphoto.

Cataloging-in-Publication Data

Names: Brundle, Harriet.
Title: Renewable energy / Harriet Brundle.
Description: New York : KidHaven Publishing, 2018. | Series: Climate change: our impact on Earth |
Includes index.
Identifiers: ISBN 9781534524736 (pbk.) | 9781534524477 (library bound) | ISBN 9781534524743
(6 pack) | ISBN 9781534524484 (ebook)
Subjects: LCSH: Renewable energy sources–Juvenile literature. | Climatic changes–Juvenile
literature.
Classification: LCC TJ808.2 B77 2018 | DDC 333.79'4–dc23

Printed in the United States of America

CPSIA compliance information: Batch #CW18KL: For further information contact Greenhaven Publishing LLC, New York, New York at 1-844-317-7404.

Please visit our website, www.greenhavenpublishing.com. For a free color catalog of all our
high-quality books, call toll free 1-844-317-7404 or fax 1-844-317-7405.

CONTENTS

PAGE 4   What Is Climate Change?

PAGE 6   What Is Nonrenewable Energy?

PAGE 8   What Is Renewable Energy?

PAGE 10   Wind Energy

PAGE 12   Solar Energy

PAGE 14   Hydropower

PAGE 16   Biofuels

PAGE 18   Geothermal Energy

PAGE 20   Problems with Renewable Energy

PAGE 22   Case Study: Renewable Energy in Norway

PAGE 24   Case Study: Energy Use in China

PAGE 26   Saving Energy at Home

PAGE 28   How Can We Help?

PAGE 30   Useful Websites

PAGE 31   Glossary

PAGE 32   Index

Words in **bold** are explained in the glossary on page 31.

CLIMATE CHANGE?

KEY TERMS

- The <u>weather</u> is the day-to-day changes we see and feel outside. For example, the weather may be sunny in the morning and rainy in the afternoon.

- The <u>climate</u> is the usual weather in a place over a longer period of time. For example, Antarctica has an extremely cold climate for most of the year.

- <u>Climate change</u> is the long-term change in the climate and usual weather patterns of an area. Climate change usually affects large areas. It could be a change in the amount of rainfall or the average temperature of an area.

Earth's climate is always changing. Over the last 4.5 billion years, Earth has experienced both hot and cold climates. For the last 11,000 years, Earth's climate has stayed at a stable temperature of around 57°F (14°C). However, in recent years this average temperature has been slowly increasing.

tropical climate

arctic climate

Why Might a Climate Change?

There are many different reasons for why a climate might change.

Some climate changes throughout history have had natural causes, for example **volcanic eruptions**. However, research has shown that changes to the climate in recent years have not been entirely related to natural causes. It is thought that a process called global warming is largely responsible.

1 Humans use energy for many different reasons, such as running our cars and powering the lights in our houses. This energy is largely produced by burning coal, oil, and natural gas. Together, these things are known as fossil fuels. When these fossil fuels are burned, they release many different gases, which are known as "greenhouse gases." One of these greenhouse gases is carbon dioxide.

2 Earth's **atmosphere** is a collection of different gases surrounding the planet. The atmosphere allows light and heat from the sun to pass through to Earth. This makes the planet warm. After this, some of the light and heat from the sun bounce off Earth, travel back through Earth's atmosphere, and go into outer space.

3 Greenhouse gases mix with the gases in Earth's atmosphere and stop the heat from the sun bouncing back into outer space. As a result, the heat gets trapped inside Earth's atmosphere and the temperature rises. The more greenhouse gases that are released into Earth's atmosphere, the hotter Earth will become.

WHAT IS NONRENEWABLE ENERGY?

Nonrenewable energy is any source of energy that will run out because it cannot **replenish** *itself in a short period of time.*

Most nonrenewable sources of energy are fossil fuels. Fossil fuels are things, such as coal, oil, and natural gas, that were formed over hundreds of millions of years. As plants and animals died, rocks and soil slowly covered them over many years. As the animals and plants became more and more tightly squeezed together, they gradually became hotter. This process turned the animal and plant remains into fossil fuels and created large underground areas that contain the fuels that we use today.

Coal is a type of fossil fuel.

This rig uses drills to access underground oil.

We use fossil fuels for several different tasks. Over the last hundred years, people have increasingly used fossil fuels, meaning that we are now running out. This is because fossil fuels take such a long time to form that we are using the fossil fuels we have faster than they can replenish. Since fossil fuels are being depleted, it is important that we find other sources of energy.

6

Glaciers are melting as a result of global warming.

Fossil fuels are an effective source of energy, but they are extremely damaging to the **environment**. As they burn, fossil fuels release carbon dioxide into the atmosphere. Carbon dioxide is a type of greenhouse gas, meaning that it contributes to global warming. Global warming is having a range of different effects on the planet, including affecting the **migration** patterns of some animals. It has also caused **glaciers** to melt. As a result, the habitats of the animals that live on these glaciers are becoming smaller. The melting ice is also causing sea levels to rise, meaning that animals that use beaches as a place to lay their eggs might soon have trouble raising their young.

The burning of fossil fuels also contributes to air pollution, which is when harmful substances are released into the air. Air pollution affects the natural world and has also been shown to make people ill.

7

WHAT IS RENEWABLE ENERGY?

Renewable energy is any type of energy that will never run out.

As nonrenewable energy sources are being used up, renewable energy is becoming more important. In our modern lives, we use a huge amount of energy every day. If we want to continue to fly around in airplanes, use smartphones, and have lights in our houses, then switching to **sustainable**, renewable energy sources must happen in the future.

Renewable energy is also known as "green" energy. This is because it does not harm the environment. Renewable energy can also be harnessed almost anywhere in the world, whereas fossil fuels can only be found in the underground areas where they were made.

It is important that we look after the environment.

In every part of the world, the need for energy is growing fast. This is partly because the population on Earth is increasing, and, as a result, there are more people who need energy. The increase in the amount of energy used is also caused by countries becoming more **developed**. For example, countries that are building more homes and businesses require more energy in order to do this.

At the moment, not enough renewable sources of energy are being used to keep up with the needs of the world. It is thought that around 15 percent of the world's energy now comes from renewable sources; however, this amount is increasing. The International Energy Agency (IEA) is a group made up of 29 countries that is seeking to increase the amount of energy produced by renewable sources. It hopes that by 2020, more than 25 percent of the energy we use will come from renewable sources.

Every year, more and more of our energy comes from renewable energy sources.

IT IS THOUGHT THAT DURING THE 21ST CENTURY, THE TOTAL AMOUNT OF ENERGY BEING USED BY THE PLANET WILL ALMOST DOUBLE.

WIND ENERGY

*Wind energy, or wind power, is when the wind is used to **generate** energy.*

Using wind energy is not a new idea; in the past, windmills were used on farms to grind grain. As the wind blows, the blades of the windmill rotate, and this generates energy that can be used by humans. If we wanted to satisfy all our energy needs just using wind power, this process would have to be performed on a much larger scale. Today, rather than small windmills, large wind **turbines** are used. They look similar to windmills, but they are much taller and the blades are much longer. The taller the wind turbine is, the more energy it can collect.

When several wind turbines are put together, it is called a wind farm. Wind farms are either built a long way out to sea or on flat, open pieces of land. This is done so that there is nothing in the way and they are exposed to as much wind as possible.

Wind turbines are typically around 13 feet (4 m) wide at the bottom and 407 feet (124 m) tall. An area must have wind speeds above 13 miles (22 km) per hour before a wind farm can be built there. As the wind blows and the blades rotate, they turn a long piece of metal called a shaft. This is connected to a **generator**. The energy produced by this generator can then be sent through wires to homes and businesses in the area.

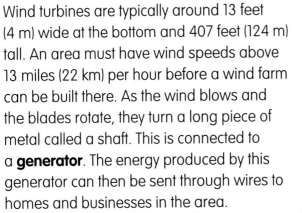

generator

California

Large wind farms can be found in countries such as China, India, England, and the United States. One of the largest wind farms in the world is in California, in the United States. It is an onshore wind farm, which means that the wind turbines have been built on land. The wind farm is called the Alta Wind Energy Center. The long-term goal for the wind farm is for it to be able to provide power to around 450,000 homes, using an estimated 600 wind turbines to do so.

11

SOLAR ENERGY

Solar energy is energy that comes from the sun's rays.

Energy from the sun has been used by humans for hundreds of years to help with tasks such as drying clothes and cooking food. In recent times, we have also been able to collect the energy in sunlight so that it can be used later. Solar energy is generated when the sun shines on solar cells, which are small **devices** that can convert the sun's rays into electrical energy. This process is already used in solar-powered watches and calculators, which all contain solar cells.

When several solar cells are grouped together, they are called solar panels. Many people place solar panels on their roofs, where they are out of the way. The solar panels are often used to heat water, which reduces the use of energy generated by burning fossil fuels.

Solar energy relies on the sun's rays.

This house is using solar energy.

When several solar panels are grouped together in one area, it is called a solar panel plant. The rows of solar panels are put in areas that receive a lot of sunlight, helping them to harness as much energy as possible. Solar panel plants are able to generate large amounts of energy because of all the solar panels working together at the same time. The International Energy Agency is hoping that within the next 50 years, solar energy could generate around 15 percent of the world's energy supply.

A solar panel plant often has many rows of solar panels.

One of the biggest issues with solar energy is that the energy provided is **inconsistent**. During the night, no electricity can be generated because there is no sunlight. For countries that are not sunny all year round, solar energy is also not suitable. Solar panels are also currently very expensive to make. As several solar panels are needed to power a home, the cost often discourages people from buying them.

HYDROPOWER

Hydropower is the name given to the process of using water to generate energy.

The movement of water has been used for many years to generate energy. In the past, the weight of falling water or fast running water was used to turn large wheels, which generated a small amount of energy.

To harness hydropower on a large scale, dams are now used. Dams are massive barriers that are built across rivers. The barriers block the flow of the river, causing a buildup of water. The water is then released in a controlled way, so that it flows quickly downward. At the bottom of the dam there is a small, underwater turbine. As the moving water hits the turbine, it rotates, and this generates electricity.

Tidal Energy

As the blades rotate, electrical energy is generated.

Tidal energy is a different type of hydropower. The ocean moves toward and away from the **shore** twice each day. This movement is called the tide. Tidal energy is generated using this movement of the world's oceans. Similarly to wind energy, turbines are used to do this. The turbines are put underwater, and as the tide moves backward and forward, the movement causes the blades of the turbine to rotate. The turbine is connected to a generator, which produces the electricity for homes and businesses in the local area.

ONE OF THE WORLD'S BIGGEST TIDAL TURBINES CAN BE FOUND OFF THE COAST OF SCOTLAND. THE TURBINE WEIGHS OVER 154 TONS (140 MT) AND GENERATES ENOUGH ELECTRICAL ENERGY TO POWER THOUSANDS OF HOMES.

BIOFUELS

*Unlike fossil fuels, which are made from animals and plants that died millions of years ago, biofuels are mostly made from plants that have been **harvested** recently.*

Different types of biofuel include wood, straw, and sugarcane. The plants that are used to make biofuels are grown specifically to make the fuel. Biofuels are renewable sources of energy because they can be replaced as quickly as they are used up, meaning that we will not run out of them. Biofuels are burned in order to generate energy.

As the plants used to make biofuels are growing, they **absorb** carbon dioxide in the air and give off oxygen. As the biofuels burn, carbon dioxide is released back into the air. However, biofuels produce less harmful chemicals than fossil fuels. This means biofuels are better for the environment than fossil fuels.

Sugarcane is used as a biofuel.

Biodiesel

Diesel is a type of fuel that is put into cars and other vehicles. When cars' engines burn the diesel to generate power, harmful gases such as carbon dioxide are released into the air. Biodiesel is an alternative to this type of fuel and is made from renewable types of oil, such as vegetable oil and rapeseed oil. A lot of biodiesel is currently made from leftover vegetable oil from restaurants and food factories.

Biodiesel is better for the environment than diesel because it does not release the same amount of harmful chemicals into the environment when it is burned. It can be used in most cars that already use diesel. However, only a few places currently sell biodiesel.

Rapeseed oil can be used to make biodiesel.

GEOTHERMAL ENERGY

There are many different layers underneath the **surface** of the earth. At the center of the earth are the inner and outer cores. The inner core is the hottest part of the earth. The temperature in the inner core reaches around 10,022°F (5,550°C). The outer core is also hot, with temperatures that are similar to the inner core. The earth's surface, or crust, is broken up into large pieces called plates. Heat from the inner and outer cores can escape through the gaps in between these plates. One example of this is a volcano.

When heat from inside the earth is used as a source of energy, it is called geothermal energy. It would be extremely difficult to use the heat directly from the inner or outer core of the earth; however, the heat that escapes to the surface can be used more easily. This escaped heat can be used for jobs such as heating water. This is a renewable type of energy because the earth's cores are always hot and will stay like this for millions of years.

Heat also escapes through hot springs, such as this one in Japan.

Tungurahua volcano, Ecuador

How Is the Earth's Heat Used?

In places where it reaches the earth's surface, geothermal heat can be used for jobs that we would have otherwise had to use fossil fuels for. One example is the heating of cold water. When cold water is pumped into the earth, it is warmed by the earth's heat. The water, which has become hot, is then pumped back out again. This means that fossil fuels do not need to be used to heat the water. In some places, water is already being heated using geothermal energy, such as in hot springs. There is also water that is deep in the earth's crust. This water has already been warmed, thanks to the temperature inside the earth, so it can be pumped to the surface and used right away.

One of the best places for geothermal energy is the "Ring of Fire," found in a **basin** in the Pacific Ocean. A large amount of the world's active volcanoes are found in the Ring of Fire, and it is a continuous source of geothermal energy.

Mt. Garibaldi
Mt. St. Helens

Aleutian trench

Kurile trench

Japan trench

Izu Ogasawara trench

Ryukyu trench

Puerto Rico trench

Philippine trench

t. Pinatubo

Mt. Mayon

Marianas trench

Middle America trench

Challenger Deep

Equator

Krakatoa

Bougainville trench

(Sunda)

Tonga trench

Peru-Chile trench

Kermadec trench

This map shows the location of the Ring of Fire in the Pacific Ocean.

PROBLEMS WITH
RENEWABLE ENERGY

At the moment, we can't rely on renewable energy to supply all the energy we need. This is partly because we cannot access and store the energy that is produced by natural sources in the same way that we can with fossil fuels. When fossil fuels are **extracted** from the earth, they can be put into containers and used when we need them. Most of the time, we can't use renewable energy sources in the same way. If, for example, the sun were to go behind a cloud, we would be unable to use its rays for energy.

Although the technology that we use to harness renewable sources of energy is constantly improving, it is currently much cheaper to generate energy using fossil fuels than it is to generate energy using renewable energy sources. For many people, using the cheapest type of energy is most important. Secondly, it is still very easy to buy fossil fuels. Although supplies are quickly running out, fossil fuels are still easy to purchase and use.

AS SUPPLIES OF FOSSIL FUELS BEGIN TO RUN LOW, THEY WILL BECOME MORE EXPENSIVE TO BUY.

Unfortunately, there are no sources of energy that do not damage the environment in some way. Although renewable sources of energy do not give off the same amount of pollution as nonrenewable sources, using all of these renewable types of energy is going to be damaging. When a wind turbine is installed, the ground must be dug up to make way for the machinery. This causes damage to that area of land. Large wind farms can therefore cause damage on a much bigger scale. When a dam is installed to harness the energy of a flowing river, it could disrupt the flow of the river and stop animals from being able to reach food in other parts of the river.

Holes must be dug into the ground before wind turbines can be installed.

Other types of renewable energy, such as geothermal energy, can only be used in certain areas. This means that for those people who do not live close to the energy source, this type of renewable energy is not an option.

21

RENEWABLE ENERGY IN NORWAY

Norway is a country in Europe, near Sweden and Finland. Norway has several different **landscapes**, including forests, rivers, and lakes. Norway has deep **valleys** that are filled with seawater. These valleys are now known as the Norwegian fjords. Norway also has a large **coastline**.

As a result of its many different landscapes, Norway is able to harness energy from a range of renewable sources. The large bodies of water in Norway mean that the country can use hydropower as a source of energy. As water flows down the mountains, the motion is used to generate energy that can be used in homes and businesses.

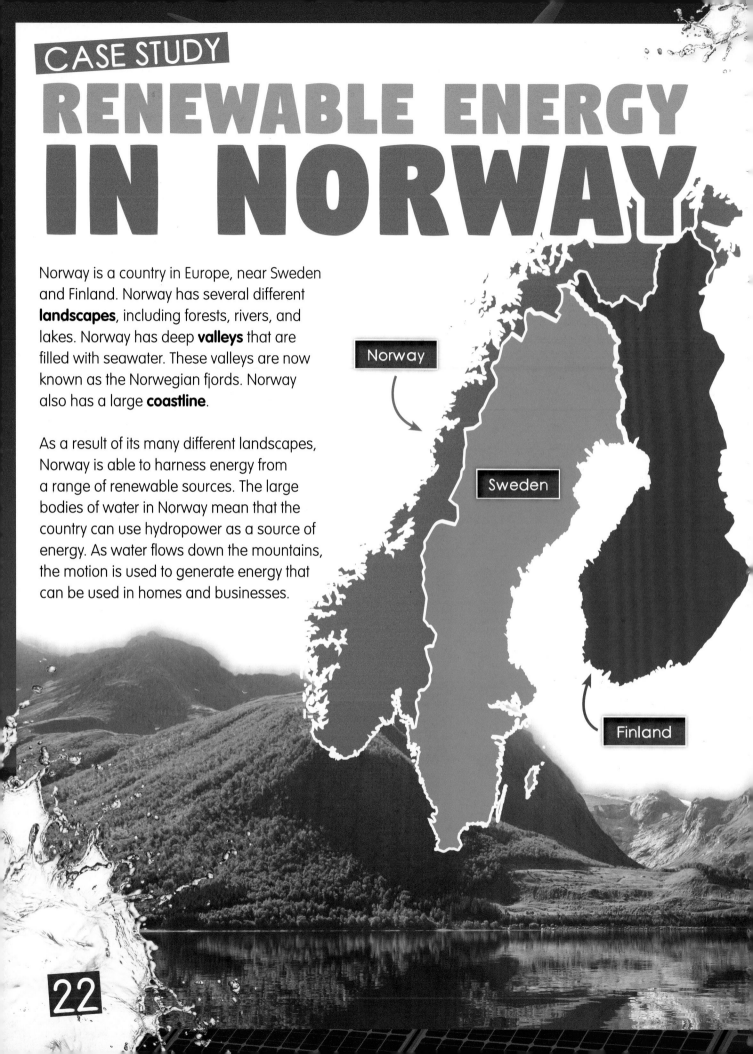

Norway

Sweden

Finland

Norway's huge coastline means that many wind turbines can be placed offshore and used to generate energy. The mountain ranges are also useful for wind energy, as they allow for wind turbines to be placed high up in areas that are not sheltered from the wind. This puts the blades on the turbines in the best position to be moved by the wind, meaning that they can generate the greatest amount of energy.

NORWAY IS ONE OF THE WORLD'S LEADING COUNTRIES IN TERMS OF ITS ELECTRIC CAR USAGE.

A large amount of the electricity used in Norway is generated using hydropower and wind energy. The country is now a world leader in terms of its renewable energy. Norway has been able to generate enough energy from renewable energy sources that it is able to sell the energy to other countries.

ENERGY USE IN CHINA

China is a country found in eastern Asia, near Russia, Mongolia, and India. For many years, the population of China has been increasing. As the population of China has grown, so has the number of houses and businesses in China. As this has happened, the amount of energy being used in China has also increased. The energy used in China is mostly generated using fossil fuels, meaning that it produces high levels of harmful greenhouse gases. This increase in the use of fossil fuels means that China has one of the highest **emission levels** of all the countries in the world.

China

Chinese flag

The **government** in China has plans that aim to reduce the amount of fossil fuels that the country uses.

The Three Gorges Dam

The Three Gorges Dam is a dam that has been built in the Yangtze River in China. The dam is the largest hydroelectric dam in the world, and it uses the flow of water coming down the river to generate energy. The dam has state-of-the-art technology that is used to harness the maximum amount of energy possible. By using hydropower rather than fossil fuels, it is hoped that the dam will help to reduce China's greenhouse gas emissions.

Since the dam has been built, however, it has had some issues. Apart from being extremely expensive to build, the dam has also caused flooding in nearby towns and cities, and many people have had to find new places to live. The dam has also damaged the environment, disrupting the flow of the river for the animals that live there. There are over 300 different types of fish living in the Yangtze River, many of which rely on traveling upstream to lay their eggs. The dam has blocked their path, making it more difficult for them to lay their eggs.

The dam has caused local areas to flood.

Yangtze River, China

Three Gorges Dam

SAVING ENERGY AT HOME

There are many different ways people can try to save energy.

It is important that we all try to reduce the amount of energy that we use, even if it comes from renewable sources. By doing this, we will help the environment and slow down the effects of climate change. Although some types of renewable energy are currently expensive, cheaper options are available.

Making homes energy **efficient** is one of the best ways to save energy. One of the best ways to make a house more energy efficient is to insulate it. When a house is insulated, lots of layers of a thick material, known as insulation, are placed inside the walls and roof. These layers of insulation make it harder for heat to escape the house. This means that less energy is needed to heat the house, as the house holds on to more heat than it did before.

Increasing the amount of insulation in a house helps to save energy.

Other ways to help save energy include turning the heating down and wearing a sweater instead. Washing your clothes at a lower temperature and drying them outside, rather than in a dryer, will also help to save energy. Items that are left plugged in but are not being used still use electricity. After you have finished using an electrical item, make sure you unplug it.

Most houses use a lot of energy; however, some houses are now being built to be energy efficient. These houses are built with well-insulated walls and ceilings and use renewable energy sources to heat the water. Rainwater is often collected and used to supply the washing machine and toilet. Although building environmentally friendly homes may cost more money to begin with, over time the people living there will save money on their energy costs.

This house is powered entirely by solar panels.

HOW CAN WE HELP?

There are many different ways that you can save energy and help to slow down climate change.

1 Think about the energy-saving tips you read on pages 26 and 27. Try to put as many of these into practice around your home as you can.

2 Tell your family and friends all about how they can save energy too! Talk to your parents about the benefits of using renewable energy sources and the small-scale changes that they could make around the house.

3 Speak to others about climate change and how important it is to look after the earth. Try to find out about **conservation** work that is happening in your area and get as many people involved as you can.

4 Recycle! It is important that we all recycle as much as we possibly can. Recycling can be done at home, at school, and in the wider community. Make sure that anything that you can recycle is taken to a recycling center or is put in a recycling bin.

Reuse anything that doesn't need to be thrown away; keep plastic bags in the cupboard, and reuse them the next time you go shopping. **5**

6 Reducing greenhouse gases will also help to slow down climate change. Rather than using a car, try to walk or bike to where you want to go. If you have to use a car, try sharing with others who are also going to the same place.

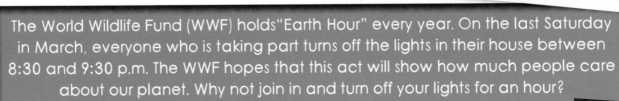

The World Wildlife Fund (WWF) holds "Earth Hour" every year. On the last Saturday in March, everyone who is taking part turns off the lights in their house between 8:30 and 9:30 p.m. The WWF hopes that this act will show how much people care about our planet. Why not join in and turn off your lights for an hour?

USEFUL WEBSITES

Go to www.earthtimes.org for interesting blogs and pages that are filled with environmentally friendly ideas and tips.

For lots of fun facts about energy, visit www.sciencekids.co.nz/sciencefacts/energy.html.

Visit www.nature.org and go to the "Where We Work" section to find out about conservation work that's happening in your area.

Take a look at www.alliantenergykids.com/EnergyandTheEnvironment/ to discover more about energy and the environment. Check out the "Fun and Games" tab for some great ideas about projects that you could try at home!

Discover more about the many different types of energy at www.kids.esdb.bg/index.html.

For tips on saving energy, take a look at http://kids.saveonenergy.ca/en/what-is-electricity/electricity-saving-tips-page-1.html.

This energy guide should be able to answer any other questions that you might have: http://tiki.oneworld.org/energy/energy.html.

GLOSSARY

absorb — to take in or soak up

atmosphere — the mixture of gases that make up the air and surround Earth

basin — a wide, rounded area of land

coastline — land that runs alongside the ocean

conservation — work that is done to protect something from damage or harm

develop — to make something advanced

device — an object designed for a particular purpose, typically machines

efficient — achieving the most while using the smallest amount of energy

emission level — an amount of air pollutant released into the atmosphere

environment — the natural world

extract — to remove or take out of something else

generate — to produce or create something, usually electricity

generator — a machine used to generate electricity

glacier — a large mass of ice that moves slowly

government — the group of people with the power to rule over a country

harvest — to gather crops

inconsistent — not the same throughout

landscape — the visible features of an area of land

migration — the seasonal movement of animals from one area to another

replenish — to fill up again

shore — the land along the edge of a large body of water

surface — the outer part of something

sustainable — able to continue over a long period of time

turbine — a machine that produces power by using fast-flowing water, steam, or air

valley — a low area of land between hills or mountains, often with a river running through it

volcanic eruption — the act of steam and other material violently leaving a volcano

INDEX

A

animals 6–7, 16, 21, 25

B

biofuel 16–17

C

California 11

carbon dioxide 5, 7, 16–17

climate 4–5, 26, 28–29

D

dams 14, 21, 25

diesel 17

E

Earth 4–5, 9, 18–20, 28–29

environment 7–8, 16–17, 21, 25–27

F

fossil fuel 5–8, 12, 16, 19–20, 24–25

G

geothermal 18–19, 21

greenhouse gas, 5, 7, 24–25, 29

H

hydropower 14–15, 22–23, 25

I

insulation 26–27

N

Norway 22–23

O

oxygen 16

P

pollution 7–8, 21

population 9, 24

R

recycling 29

S

Scotland 15

solar 12–13, 27

T

temperature 4–5, 18–19, 27

tides 15

turbines 10–11, 14–15, 21, 23

V

volcanoes 18–19

W

water 8, 12, 14–15, 18–19, 22, 25, 27

weather 4

wind 8, 10–11, 15, 21, 23

wind farms 10–11, 21